THE AMERICAN HERITAGE SERIES

S0-AFC-806

This Is My America

A Declaration of Dependence

Arranged by

RICHARD KINGSMORE

CONTENTS

PART I
O Say Can You See

with
My Country, 'Tis of Thee

Words and Music by
DARYL K. WILLIAMS
Arranged by Richard Kingsmore

4

*"My Country, 'Tis of Thee"

My coun - try, 'tis of thee, Sweet land of lib - er - ty, Of thee I sing.

CD: 3 / 34

*NARRATOR: Fourscore and seven years ago, our fathers brought forth upon this continent a new nation, conceived in liberty, and dedicated to the

proposition that all men are created equal…we here highly resolve, that this nation, under God, shall have a new birth of freedom, and that government of

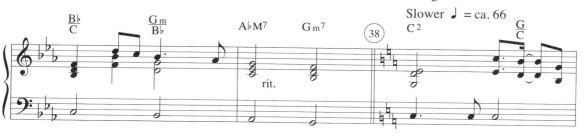

the people, by the people, and for the people shall not perish from the earth.
(From the "Gettysburg Address", Abraham Lincoln)

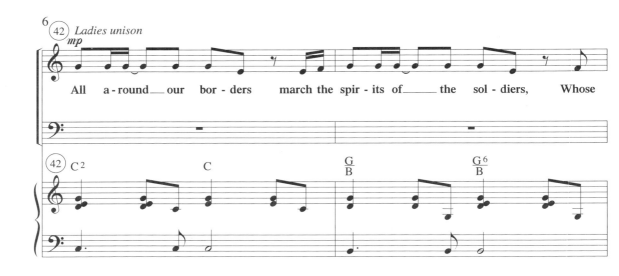

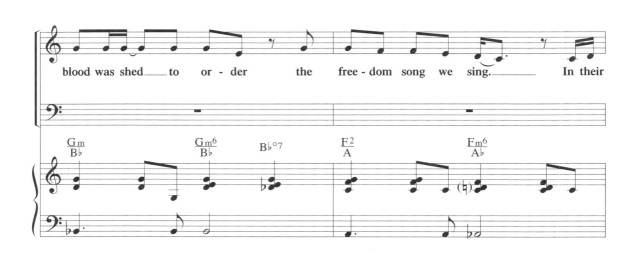

say can you see it's not too late___ for pray - ing, A -

mer - i - ca's___ worth sav - ing. O___ say can you see.

War has now in-vad-ed what was once con-sid-ered sa-cred. With

crime the bat-tle rag-es here in the U. S. A. In our

schools there are chil-dren dy-ing where stars and stripes are fly-ing. But our

12

PART II
This Is My America

with

You're a Grand Old Flag
The Star-spangled Banner
God of Our Fathers
The Battle Hymn of the Republic

Words and Music by
CHRIS MACHEN
Arranged by Richard Kingsmore

16

18

nev - er a boast or brag. But should auld ac-quaint-ance

be for-got, Keep your eye on the grand old flag.

CD: 12 / 43

*Narrator begins

*NARRATOR: Please stand as we say the "Pledge of Allegiance."

NARRATOR, CHOIR and CONGREGATION: I pledge allegiance to the flag of the United States of America and to the Republic for which it stands: one Nation under God, indivisible, with liberty and justice for all.

*"The Star-spangled Banner"

free_____ and the home

67 **CD: 14 / 45**   Faster ♩ = ca. 112

of   the   brave?

70 *Unison* *mf*

This   is   my   A - mer - i - ca,   Where in

Unison *mf*

70 Db   Gb/Db   Db   Ab/C

mf   simile

love   Comes from God's own hand   to this pil - grim land, This is

my   A - mer - i - ca.

CD: 15 / 46

flowing   decresc.

*Narrator begins

mp

*NARRATOR: Benjamin Franklin said, "The longer I live the more convincing proof I see of this truth: that God governs in the affairs of men and if a sparrow cannot fall to the ground without His notice, is it probable that an empire can rise without His aid? We have been assured in the sacred writings that except the Lord build the house, they labor in vain that build it."

CD: 16 / 47

*"God of Our Fathers"

God of our fa - thers, whose al - might - y

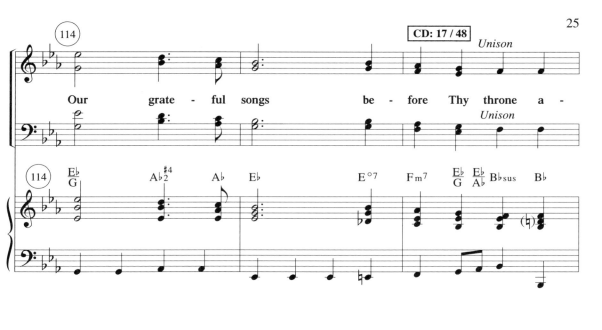

*NARRATOR: Abraham Lincoln said, "It is the duty of nations as well as of men to own their dependence upon the over-ruling power of God and to recognize the sublime truth announced in the Holy Scriptures that those nations only are blessed whose God is the Lord."

CD: 18 / 49

Thy love di-vine hath led us in the

past. In this free land by

146 Unison

way. This is my A-

146

F   Ebm9   Absus   Ab   Db   Gb/Db   Db

mer - i - ca,   Where free - dom's price was   paid   By the

Ab/C   simile   Gb/Bb   Db/Ab   Gb   Ab/Gb   Db/F   Absus/Eb   Db

150

ones   who   died   with a   pa - triot's   pride,   What a   sac - ri - fice   was

Divisi

150   F7sus/C   Cm7   F   Eb/F   F   Bbm   Bb4/2   Bbm/Ab   Eb7/G   Eb13   Eb7

*"The Battle Hymn of the Republic"

not for-get the sac-ri-fi-ces made for you and me. For the ones who died for free-dom, and the

PART III
Come Home America

with

America, the Beautiful

Words and Music by
CHRIS MACHEN
Arranged by Richard Kingsmore

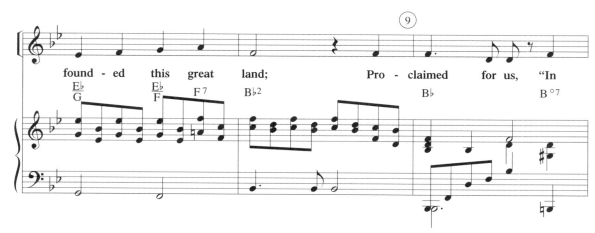

came from for-eign lands___ a-cross the o-cean   In

search of some-where they could call___ their own.   To

wor-ship God in free - dom was their pas-sion.   A

CD: 25 / 56

love so strong it drove___ them from their home.

dies.

Db2

46 *mf*
Thro' the years___ our lib - er - ty___ was threat - ened___ And

Choir
mp
Oo___
mp

46 D 2   D   G 2/D
mf

men have died de-fend - ing free-dom's right. But

Oo

CD: 27 / 58

day by day our en - e - my is chang-ing Our

free - dom is the foe_____ that we must fight.

Un - re - strained we kill the un - born ba - bies._____ De -

Ah,_____

Eb2   Ebsus

CD: 28 / 59

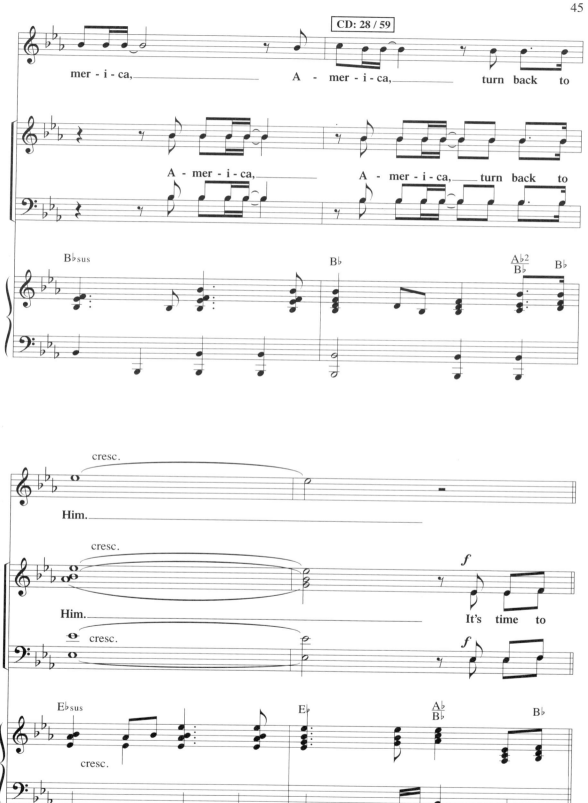

turn back, come home A - mer - i - ca _____ To the

place where faith in God ____ lights our way. It's time to

turn back, come home A - mer - i - ca _____ And re-

48

THIS IS MY AMERICA

This Is My America

A Declaration of Dependence

This Is My America

A Declaration of Dependence

This Is My America

A Declaration of Dependence

This Is My America

A Declaration of Dependence

This Is My America

A Declaration of Dependence